Lost in Egypt
Nick Hunter

Contents

Northcott School

Joel's Journal

Joel Trotter
Age 8

The Trotter family

Our cousin Reema is always cool and calm.

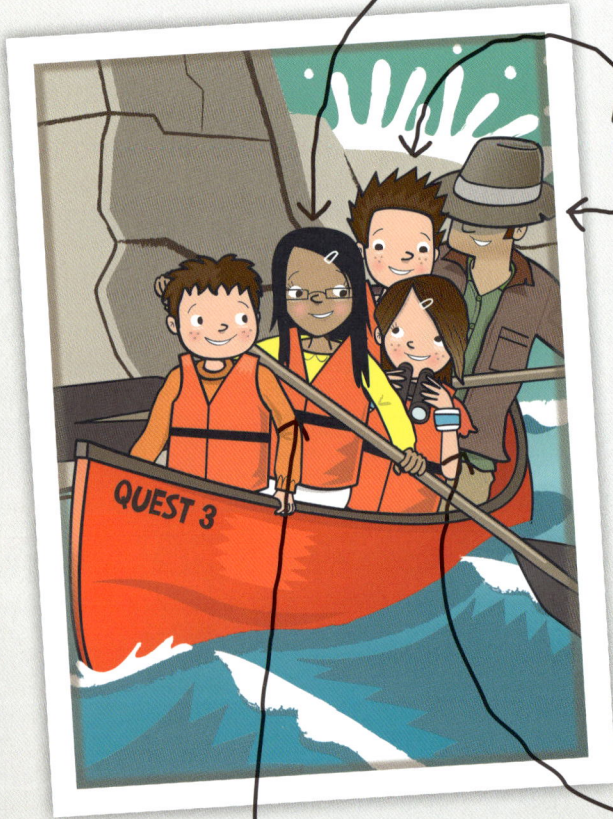

My older brother Zac knows lots of stuff.

Uncle Globe is Dad's older brother. He has loads of adventures. Dad says Globe is just a big kid.

QUEST 3

I'm Joel — the youngest and the noisiest.

Ruth bosses me and Zac around.

Thursday 7th October

Guess what! I got an email from Uncle Globe today. He's in Egypt!

From: Globetrotter
To: Joel Trotter
Sent: 7th October 11:35
Subject: A puzzle

Hi Joel,

I'm sending this from Cairo, Egypt. My friend Dr Rosie Stone works here as an expert on ancient Egypt. She asked me to return something to her. It's a necklace with some kind of creepy-crawly on it. I've included a picture.

The problem is, Rosie isn't here to meet me – she seems to have disappeared! Can you help me find out what the necklace is for, and where I need to take it? I've enclosed a book which might help. I'll send you some questions along the way. Let me know what you find out.

Mummy's the word!

Globe

P.S. There may be a reward for your help.

Great! A real mystery to solve. I can't wait to find out about ancient Egypt. I'll start reading!

Ancient Egypt

Ancient and modern

The modern country of Egypt in North Africa has an amazing history. Anyone travelling around modern Egypt can see ruined **temples** and palaces. The ruined temples were built by the people of ancient Egypt. The **civilization** they built began more than 5000 years ago and lasted for 3000 years.

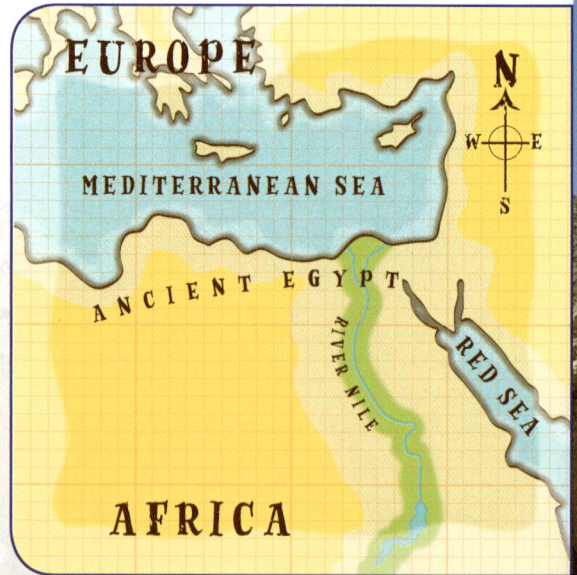

EUROPE

MEDITERRANEAN SEA

ANCIENT EGYPT

RIVER NILE

RED SEA

AFRICA

N
W E
S

BC

Timeline

0   **A**

3100: Ancient Egypt united under one king.

2686–2181: Old Kingdom

2040-1786: Middle Kingdom

1570-1070: New Kingdom

30: Egypt becomes part of Roman Empire – the end of ancient Egypt

The Temple of Amun at Karnak. Construction of temples at Karnak began during the Middle Kingdom.

The Great Pyramid at Giza was built in around 2600 BC.

The kings or **pharaohs** of the New Kingdom built **tombs** in the Valley of the Kings.

In which year did the ancient kingdom of Egypt come to an end?
Globe

The Mighty River Nile

In the 'black land'

Ancient Egypt could not have existed without the River Nile. Every year the Nile flooded the area around the river. The Egyptians called this the 'black land'.

Most Egyptians lived close to the river. The flood meant that this land could be used to grow food. The area away from the river was hot desert.

Flood warning

The Nile flood was not always the same. If the flood was too high, towns and crops would be washed away. If the flood was too low, not enough food could be grown and people would starve.

Nile facts

- Length: 4160 miles (6695 km) – the world's longest river
- Flows through eastern Africa to the Mediterranean Sea
- Floods from July to September

Where did people live in ancient Egypt?
Globe

Beyond the Nile

The 'red land'

Outside the Nile Valley was desert, or the 'red land'. This land was so hot and dry that nothing could grow there. However, the Egyptians did find metals and other **minerals** that they could use to make tools and jewellery.

The deserts of ancient Egypt were also home to scorpions.

Did you know?

In ancient times, lions and cheetahs probably roamed the 'red land'.

Egypt is mostly made up of desert.

The sun and the scarab

Ancient Egyptians were obsessed with the sun. The sun came up every morning to bring heat and light to grow their crops. When it went down in the evening, the land became very cold. Egyptian paintings show the sun being pushed across the sky by a giant **scarab** beetle.

The scarab beetle rolls balls of dung from dung heaps. This is where the Egyptians got their idea that a giant scarab beetle pushed the sun across the sky.

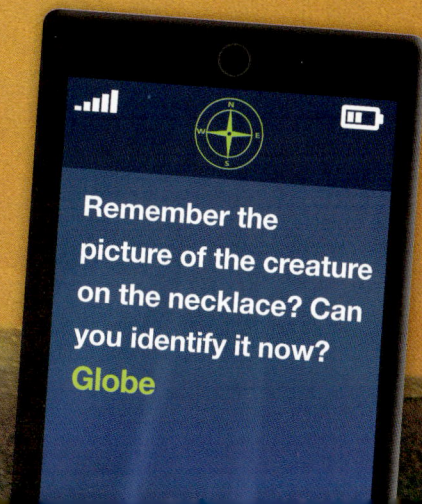

Remember the picture of the creature on the necklace? Can you identify it now? **Globe**

Journey to the Pyramids

Monday 11th October

Monday morning again. I've learnt lots about ancient Egypt. I'll email Globe and let him know what I've found out:

* The ancient Egyptians lived more than 2000 years ago. The Romans took over in 30 BC.

* The River Nile was very important. It could be part of Globe's journey.

* The bug on the necklace could be a scarab beetle. Scarab beetles were a big deal in ancient Egypt.

Hi Joel,

Thanks for your help. I think the necklace might be a scarab beetle too. It must be very old and valuable so I really need to give it back to Rosie! Someone told me Rosie might have gone to the pyramids. Tomorrow I'm going there to look for her. Can you find out more about them?

Let me know what you sphinx!

Globe

My transport to the pyramids!

If the necklace is from ancient Egypt it must be thousands of years old — even older than one of Zac's jokes! I wonder who it could have belonged to. I hope Globe's looking after it.

The Pyramids

How did they do that?

Imagine a building made up of more than 2 million blocks of stone. Each block weighs about three tonnes. The blocks have to be moved into position without using cranes or trucks. The ancient Egyptians did all this when they built the pyramids of Egypt.

For many centuries, no one could work out how the pyramids of Egypt were built. Thousands of people must have worked to move the huge stones into place.

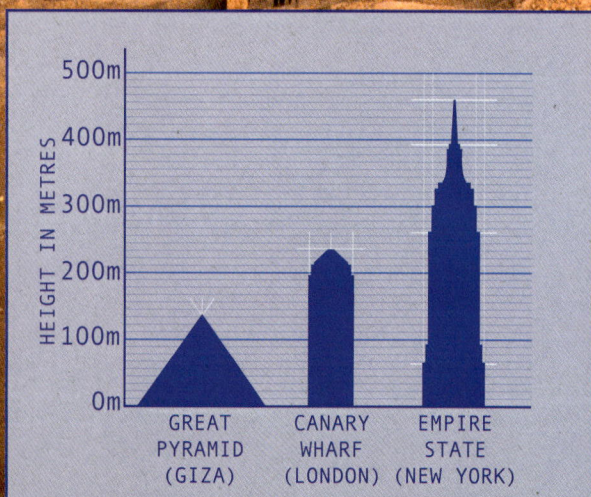

The Great Pyramid at Giza was the world's tallest building for more than 3500 years.

HEIGHT IN METRES

500m
400m
300m
200m
100m
0m

GREAT PYRAMID (GIZA)

CANARY WHARF (LONDON)

EMPIRE STATE (NEW YORK)

Why were they built?

The pyramids were built as tombs for Egyptian kings, or pharaohs. The tombs were so huge because the ancient Egyptians believed their king, or pharaoh, was almost a god. The Great Pyramid was built for a king called Khufu.

In the middle of each pyramid is a burial chamber.

The pyramids are amazing. But what is in the middle of each pyramid?
Globe

Religion and Gods

Gods for everything

The ancient Egyptians had thousands of gods. Many of the gods were shown as people with the heads of animals. Here are just a few of them:

Name	Appearance	Details
Horus	Man with the head of a hawk	Protected the pharaoh
Hathor	Woman with cow's horns	Wife of Horus, goddess of love
Isis	Woman with headdress shaped like a throne	Mother of Horus, protected people in need
Khepri	Man with the head of a scarab beetle	Controlled the movement of the sun

Horus

Hathor

Isis

Khepri

Amulets for protection

The ancient Egyptians thought bad things would happen if they did not please the gods. People often wore **amulets** with pictures of gods on them. They thought these necklaces or pieces of jewellery would protect them.

A painting of the Egyptian god Khepri

Which god do you think the scarab necklace was trying to please?
Globe

Learning the Language

Reading and writing

The best way to be rich and important in ancient Egypt was to learn how to write. The ancient Egyptians had a very complicated system of writing called **hieroglyphs**. The only people who could read and write were **scribes**. This meant they were very powerful.

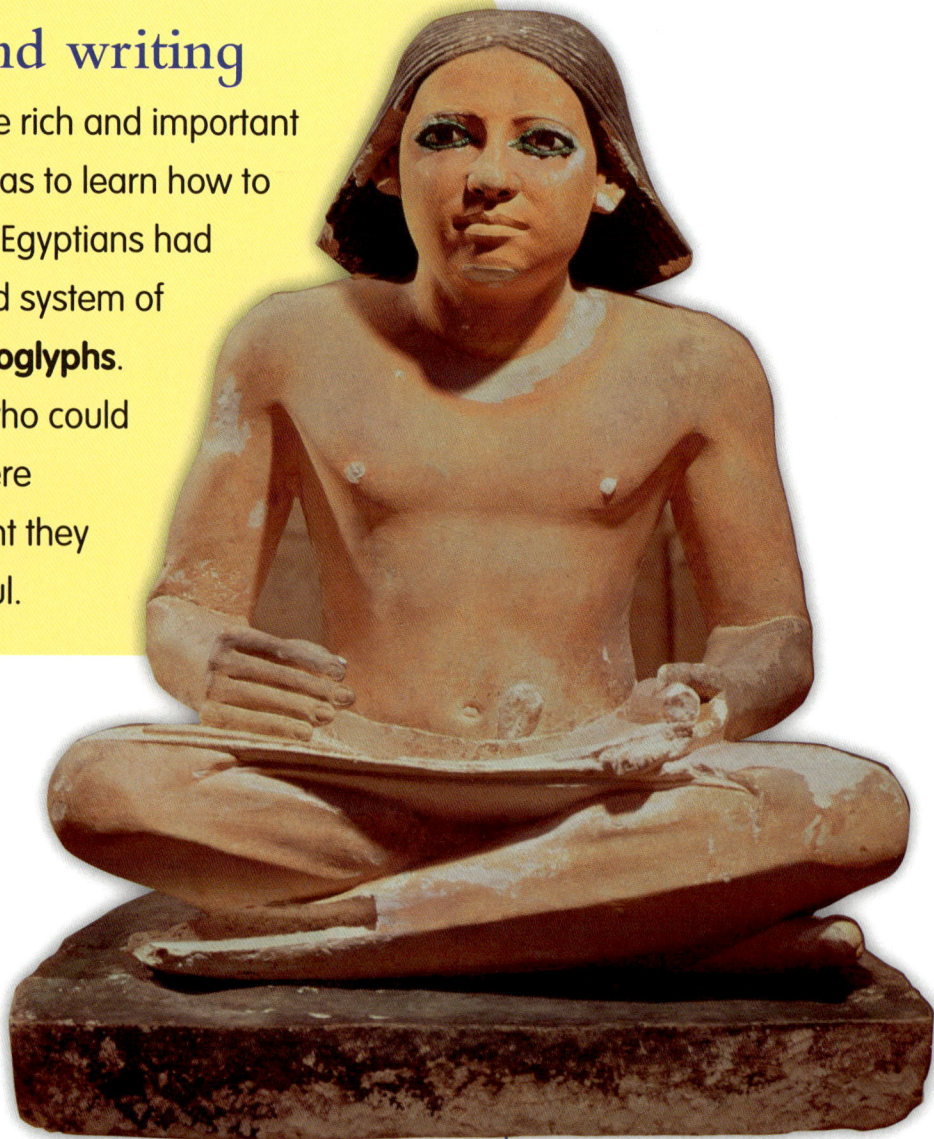

Did you know?

To understand hieroglyphs, scribes needed to learn about 1000 different symbols.

Scribes may have made hieroglyphs really difficult to understand so ordinary people could not read them.

Understanding hieroglyphs

We can understand hieroglyphs because of an amazing discovery in 1799. The Rosetta Stone is a piece of rock with words carved on it in both Egyptian hieroglyphs and ancient Greek. Because people could understand ancient Greek, they were able to work out what the hieroglyphs meant.

River

Scribe

King or pharaoh

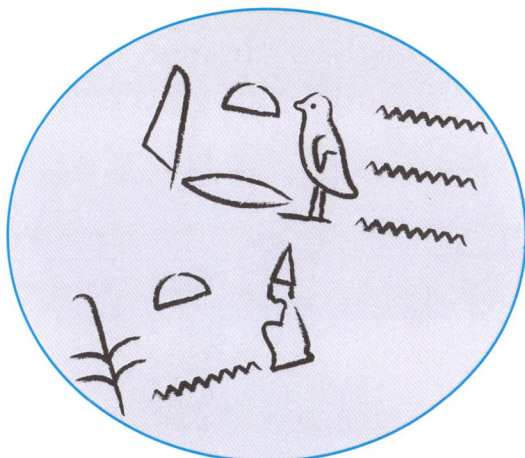

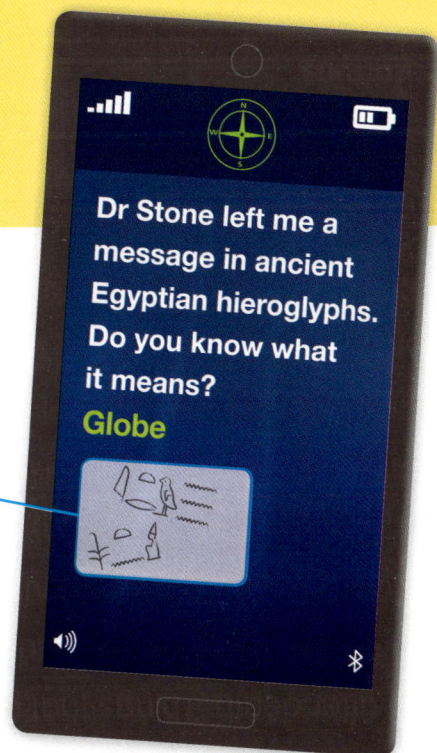

Dr Stone left me a message in ancient Egyptian hieroglyphs. Do you know what it means?
Globe

HIEROGLYPHIC ALPHABET

A Close Shave

Thursday 14th October

The more I find out about ancient Egypt, the more amazing it seems. The necklace sounds like it might be an amulet. It probably belonged to someone rich and powerful, like a scribe or even a king. It must be worth a fortune.

Friday 15th October

I must also tell Globe that I know what Rosie Stone's message means. The two hieroglyphs mean 'river' and 'king'. Maybe she wants him to go up the river and meet a king. So why didn't she just tell him that?

From: Globetrotter
To: Joel Trotter
Sent: 15th October 19:25
Subject: Challenge

Hi Joel,

Thanks for decoding Rosie's message. She wasn't there when I went to the pyramids. I think she knows something I don't. That's why she's leaving secret messages. Someone tried to take the necklace out of my pocket when I was on the way to the pyramids. I stopped him just in time and he ran off. It seems more than one person wants the necklace.

I'm off up the Nile. Do you know where I can find a king?

Globe

My boat, the 'Nefertiti'

That was a lucky escape. I hope the amulet keeps Globe safe. I'll see what I can find out about kings.

Life on the River

Travelling by boat

The yearly flood was not the only reason why the Nile was important to ancient Egyptians. Most people did not travel far. If they did, they went by boat along the river. Water for drinking also came from the river.

This is a model of the boats Egyptians used to travel along the River Nile.

Dangers of the Nile

The Nile crocodile is one of the biggest dangers of the River Nile. Its strength and large teeth make it just as much of a danger now as it was to the ancient Egyptians.

Uniting Egypt's people

The river linked Lower and Upper Egypt. Lower Egypt was the area close to the Mediterranean Sea. Upper Egypt was home to the kings of the **New Kingdom**. These kings built temples and tombs.

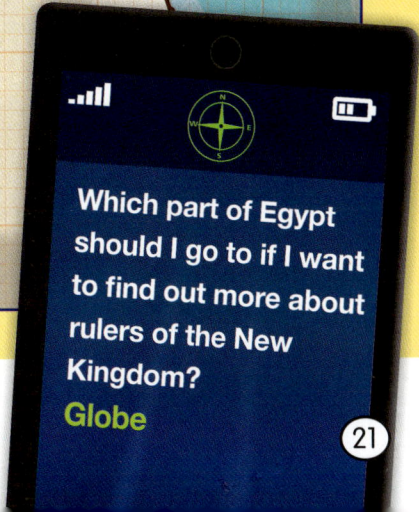

Mediterranean Sea

LOWER EGYPT

CAIRO

PYRAMIDS

MEMPHIS

RIVER NILE

N
W — E
S

Red Sea

TEMPLE AT LUXOR

TEMPLE OF AMUN AT KARNAK

THEBES

VALLEY OF THE KINGS

UPPER EGYPT

Which part of Egypt should I go to if I want to find out more about rulers of the New Kingdom?
Globe

Discovering Temples

Temples, not tombs

The ancient Egyptians built temples to honour their gods. One of the largest is the temple of Amun at Karnak. Although kings ordered the temples to be built, their tombs were actually elsewhere.

Did you know?

The temple at Karnak is one of the biggest temples ever built. The pillars inside the temple are so massive that 50 people could stand together on top of one of them.

The Avenue of **Sphinxes** at the temple at Karnak.

Inside the temple

Ordinary Egyptians would enter the temple grounds on festival days through a decorated gateway or **pylon**. Statues and carvings would show the king who built the temple and scenes of gods and goddesses. Only the priests and the king himself could go inside the temple. At its heart was the **sanctuary** with a statue of the temple's god.

Priests cleaned the temple statue and offered it food to keep the god happy.

Are the kings buried in the temples at Thebes?
Globe

The Afterlife

Life after death

The ancient Egyptians believed that people lived on after death. Things that people might need in the **afterlife** were buried with them. For richer people, this could include models of the things they owned, even including servants.

Making mummies

Egyptians would also need their bodies in the afterlife. When wealthy people died, their bodies were preserved as **mummies**.

The mummy and mummy case of an ancient Egyptian princess

The mummy case was carved and painted to look like the person inside.

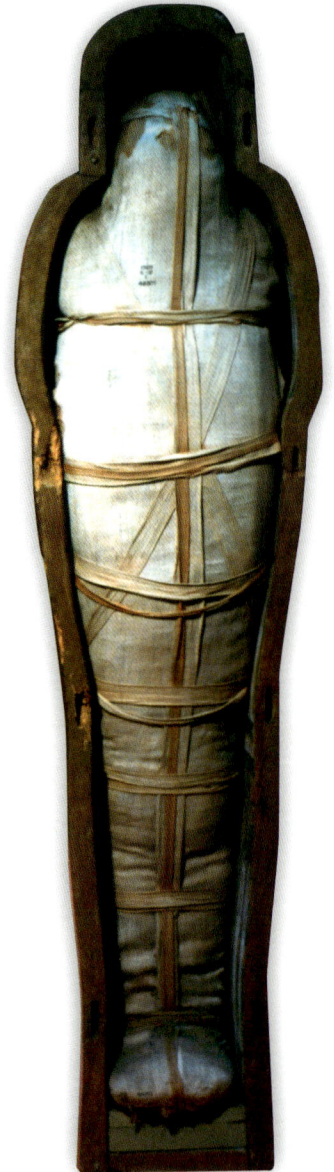

How to make a mummy

1. Remove the dead person's brain and **internal organs.**

2. Dry out the body for several weeks using **natron.**

3. Wrap it in strips of **linen.**

4. Place it in a decorated coffin.

Did you know?

The only organ that would not be removed during mummification was the heart, because the Egyptians believed that the soul of the person lived there. A carved scarab would be placed over the heart.

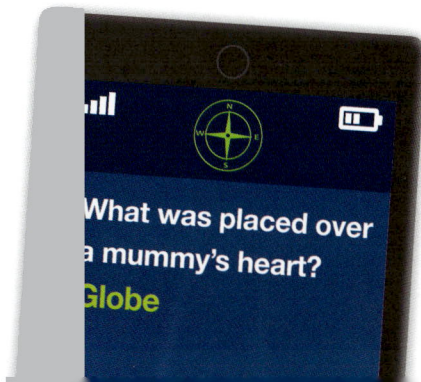

Sacred animals like cats were also mummified.

What was placed over a mummy's heart?

Globe

Amazing Discoveries

Tutankhamen's tomb

In 1922 Howard Carter made an amazing discovery. He and his team found the tomb of a young king called Tutankhamen, who had died in about 1325 BC. Inside the tomb, they found the king's mummified body.

Tutankhamen's tomb was full of treasures that had been buried with him, like this scarab bracelet.

Mysterious death

Tutankhamen was only about 18 years old when he died. Some people who have studied his body think that he may have been murdered. Others think he died from a fall or an illness.

Top tombs

This tomb was the most amazing discovery in an area called the Valley of the Kings. The kings of ancient Egypt's New Kingdom were buried there. Queens were buried nearby in the Valley of the Queens.

Tomb robbers

Many of the tombs in the Valley of the Kings have been raided by tomb robbers over thousands of years. Precious things from these tombs have been lost forever.

This golden mask was placed over Tutankhamen's face when he was buried.

Where were the kings buried?
Globe

Secrets of the valley

Wednesday 20th October

I think Globe needs to meet Dr Stone in the Valley of the Kings. Maybe the amulet belonged to a king. I'll send Globe a message now.

POST CARD

Hi Joel,

Thanks for guiding me to the Valley of the Kings. I told Rosie all about you. She's really happy to have the amulet back. She doesn't know if it actually belonged to a king but it tells us a lot about the ancient Egyptians.

I've got your reward. Your sister Ruth may not like it.

Nile be home soon,

Globe

Joel Trotter,
3100 Temple Road,
Oxford, UK

50c
POSTAGE

Postcard

TRAVEL

Saturday 23rd October

Globe's back from Egypt and the scarab amulet is in a museum where it belongs. Globe found out that the people who were trying to steal it wanted to keep it for themselves. They thought it would bring them luck.

Globe brought me a present - my own scarab amulet! It's not real but it's a good copy. It looked real enough to make Ruth scream when I put it on her bed! Globe said she wouldn't like it.

Scarabs and the Sun

Monday 25th October

Back to school! Mrs Pankhurst asked us to do a report on ancient Egypt. When I said mine was about dung beetles, she didn't seem too keen. 'Trust me,' I said. 'It's more interesting than it sounds.'

✓ Well done! ☺

The scarab beetle

The dung beetle, or scarab beetle, was very important to the ancient Egyptians. The ancient Egyptians believed that the sun was pushed across the sky every day by a giant scarab beetle. They even had a god called Khepri whose head was in the shape of a scarab beetle.

Why did they believe this?

The scarab beetle rolls balls of dung into its burrow. The Egyptians thought the ball was like the sun.

page 1 of 2

30

How do we know?

The Egyptians thought they would be reborn after they died, just like the sun was reborn every morning. People have found amulets and other objects showing scarab beetles in Egyptian tombs. Scarabs on amulets brought luck.

page 2 of 2

Mrs Pankhurst liked the report a lot, so maybe my amulet really is going to bring me luck!

Glossary

afterlife after someone died, ancient Egyptians believed they would be reborn in the afterlife

amulet magic charm worn to bring good luck or ward off evil

civilization society where people live in settled communities and live in a certain way

hieroglyph picture symbol used in ancient Egyptian writing

internal organs parts inside the body that perform particular tasks, such as lungs and liver

linen a type of cloth

minerals substances like metals and rocks that are found in nature but are not living things

mummy body that has been treated with chemicals and wrapped in linen so it does not decay after death

natron a type of salt which was used to dry out bodies to prepare them for mummification

New Kingdom period between 1570 and 1070 BC when ancient Egypt was ruled by kings in Upper Egypt

pharaoh the title of the kings of ancient Egypt

pylon gateway of an Egyptian temple

sanctuary part of a temple containing the statue of the god

scarab (beetle) type of insect sacred in ancient Egypt, also known as a dung beetle

scribe person who could read and write hieroglyphs

sphinx mythological creature with the body of a lion and the head of a human

temple building where a god was worshipped

tomb grave. In ancient Egypt, a person's tomb contained what they needed for the afterlife

Index

MY CLASS
LOOKS AFTER
PETS

আমার ক্লাস
পোষা জন্তুদের
যত্ন করে।

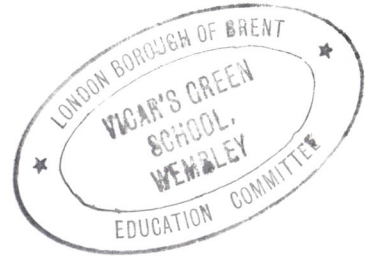

My class
looks after
pets

আমার ক্লাস
পোষা জন্তুদের
যত্ন করে।

Photography:
Chris Fairclough

ফোটোগ্রাফী:—
ক্রীস্‌ ফেয়ারক্লাফ

Translation:
ELB Translation
Services Ltd

অনুবাদ: ই এল্‌ বি ট্র্যান্‌স্‌লেশন
সার্ভিসেস লিমিটেড

Vicki Lee
meets
Martin Cox

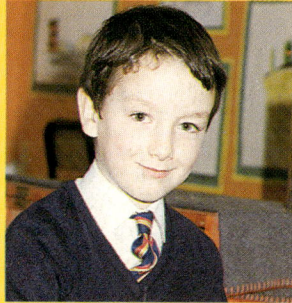

ভিকিলী মার্টিন
কক্সের সাথে
দেখা করেছে।

Franklin Watts
London/New York/Toronto/Sydney

Every morning,
our caretaker takes his dog
for a walk.
If we see him, we wave.

প্রত্যেকদিন সকালে
আমাদের বাড়ীর রক্ষক তার কুকুরকে
হাঁটাতে নিয়ে যায় ।
আমরা তাকে দেখলে হাত নেড়ে অভিনন্দন জানাই ।

Where we live, it would be hard for some of us to keep a cat or a dog.

আমরা যেখানে থাকি সেখানে আমাদের কারো কারো পক্ষে কুকুর কিংবা বিড়াল রাখার অসুবিধা ।

But in my school
we have lots of small pets
that we all look after.

কিন্তু আমাদের স্কুলে অনেক ছোট
পোষা জন্তু আছে যাদের আমরা
দেখাশোনা করি ।

In my classroom
are some baby hamsters.

আমার ক্লাসে কয়েকটা বাচ্চা
হ্যামস্টার আছে ।

Now they are chubby and furry. They were like little pink sausages when they were born.

এখন ওরা বেশ নাদুস নুদুস আর লোমশ । ওদের যখন জন্ম হয়েছিল তখন ওদের ছোট গোলাপী সসেজের মত দেখাচ্ছিল ।

Our gerbil lives in a nest
of paper strips.
He is always trying to get out.

আমাদের জারবিল কাগজের ফালির
বাসায় থাকে ।
সে সব সময় বেরিয়ে আসতে চায় ।

His feet tickle Matthew's hands.
Sometimes the gerbil nips
with his tiny teeth,
but it doesn't really hurt.

ওর পা ম্যাথুর হাতে সুড়সুড়ি দেয় ।
কখনও কখনও জারবিল ওর ছোট দাঁত
দিয়ে কামড়ায় কিন্তু তাতে
খুব একটা ব্যথা লাগে না ।

Raffles, the rabbit lives
in a hutch lined with straw.
We leave it open
so he can come out.

রাফেলস্ নামে খরগোশটি একটি খড়
বিছানো খাঁচায় থাকে ।
আমরা খাঁচাটি খুলে রাখি যাতে
সে বেরিয়ে আসতে পারে ।

I love to stroke his silky fur.

আমি ওর রেশমী লোমে হাত বুলাতে ভালবাসি ।

He is heavy to hold.
He kicks with his back legs
and wiggles,
but I hold him
so that he feels safe.

ওকে তুলে ধরতে বেশ ভারী লাগে ।
ও ওর পিছনের পা দিয়ে লাথি
দেয় আর এদিক ওদিক নড়াচড়া
করে কিন্তু আমি ওকে ধরে থাকি
যাতে ও নিরাপদ মনে করে ।

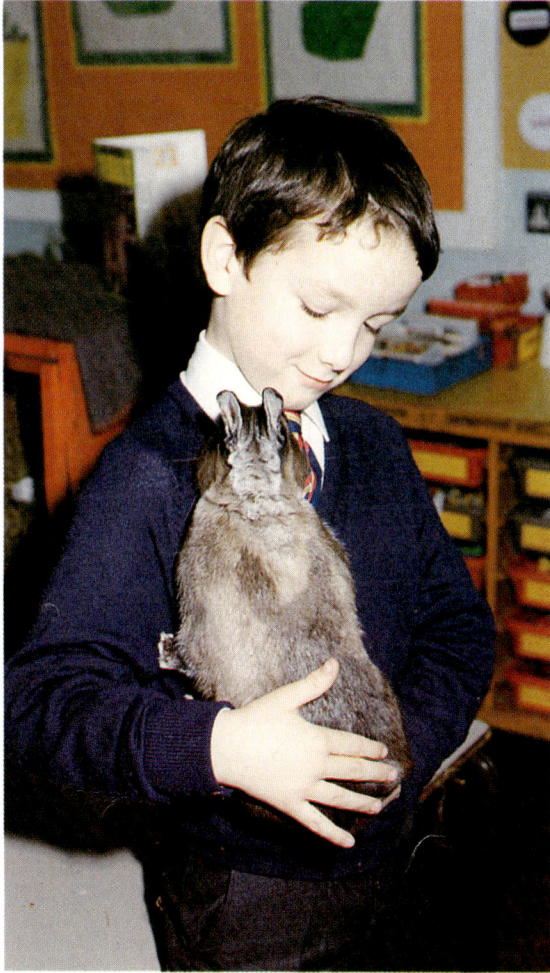

I feed him rabbit mix every day.
We buy his food from the zoo.
It looks like tiny logs.

আমি ওকে রোজ খরগোশের খাবার দিই ।
আমরা ওর খাবার চিড়িয়াখানা থেকে কিনি ।
এই খাবার ছোট ছোট কাঠের গুঁড়ির
মত দেখতে ।

We watch him to see how he moves.

আমরা ওর দিকে তাকিয়ে লক্ষ্য রাখি
ও কেমন করে নড়াচড়া করে ।

We give him carrot and cabbage
to see if he likes them.

আমরা ওকে গাজর আর বাঁধাকপি দিয়ে
দেখি ও সেগুলি পছন্দ করে কিনা ।

Then we write about what we saw.

তারপর আমরা যা দেখেছি তার
বিবরণ লিখি ।

Raffles nose goes up and down. He Licks his paw. He Jumps up and down. His ears go side to side. Paul

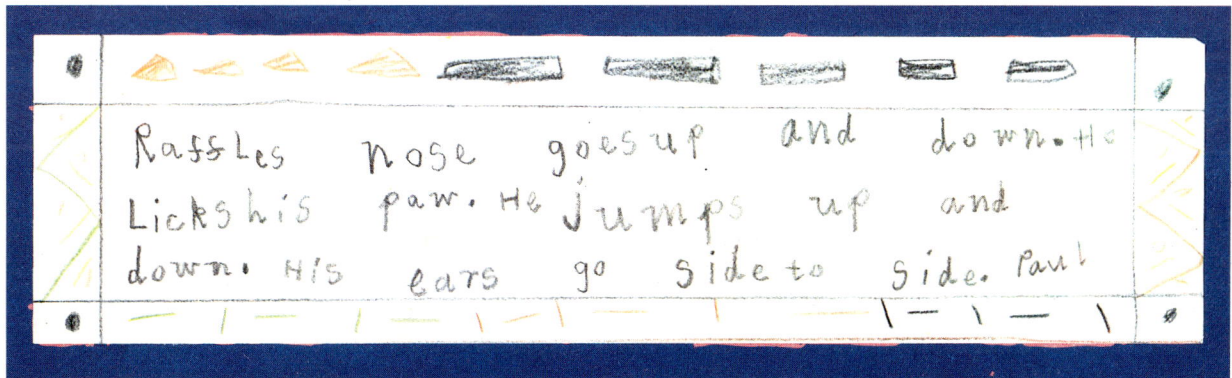

We draw pictures
and write stories about him.

আমরা ওর ছবি আঁকি আর ওকে
নিয়ে গল্প রচনা করি।

One of my friends prints
a picture of Raffles.

আমাদের এক বন্ধু রাফেলসের
একটি ছবি ছাপিয়েছে ।

Some of my friends make
clay models of our pets.

আমাদের কোন কোন বন্ধু মাটি দিয়ে আমাদের
এই পোষা জন্তুদের মূর্তি তৈরী করেছে ।

The older children have made
these models of their rabbit.

বড় বড় ছেলেমেয়েরা মাটি দিয়ে তাদের
খরগোশের আকার তৈরী করেছে ।

At hometime, I clean out
Raffles' straw.
Sometimes it's a bit smelly.

আমার অবসর সময়ে রাফেলসের
খড় পরিষ্কার করি ।
এক এক সময় একটু দুর্গন্ধ হয় ।

I make sure he has food and water.
Then I tidy up.

ওর খাবার ও জলের যোগানের দিকে
আমি সবসময় লক্ষ্য রাখি ।
তারপর আমি সব গুছিয়ে রাখি ।

He leaps back into his hutch,
but he can hop out later
when it is quiet.

ও লাফ দিয়ে আবার নিজের খাঁচায় চলে যায়
কিন্তু পরে চারদিক শান্ত হলে ও আবার
একপায়ে লাফ দিয়ে বেরিয়ে আসতে পারে ।

I'll see him tomorrow.

আগামীকাল আমি আবার ওকে দেখবো ।

© 1986 Franklin Watts
12A Golden Square
London W1R 4BA

ISBN 0 86313 557 9

Editor: Ruth Thomson
Design: Edward Kinsey

Printed in Belgium

The Publishers, author and photographer would like to thank the staff and pupils of Hampden Gurney Church of England Junior Mixed and Infant School, London W1. Special thanks are due to Father Michael Burgess, Jean Telfer and Teresa Barclay.

Vicki Lee is Professional Assistant in Education Service of the London Borough of Ealing.